AF116909

Idyllic

Andrew La Balak | Dyñel Ortiz |
Sweet Cold Ruth | Sol de Litras

Ukiyoto Publishing

All global publishing rights are held by

Ukiyoto Publishing

Published in 2024

Content Copyright © Litras Community

Isbn 9789362698018

All rights reserved.

No part of this publication may be reproduced, transmitted, or stored in a retrieval system, in any form by any means, electronic, mechanical, photocopying, recording or otherwise, without the prior permission of the publisher.

The moral rights of the author have been asserted.

This is a work of fiction. Names, characters, businesses, places, events, locales, and incidents are either the products of the author's imagination or used in a fictitious manner. Any resemblance to actual persons, living or dead, or actual events is purely coincidental.

This book is sold subject to the condition that it shall not by way of trade or otherwise, be lent, resold, hired out or otherwise circulated, without the publisher's prior consent, in any form of binding or cover other than that in which it is published.

www.ukiyoto.com

Dedication

To all our awesome peeps out there – our fam, our special someone's, pals, cousins, classmates, work buddies, squad members, churchmates, and yes, even our coffee pals.

Big shoutout to those crushes who ghosted us, and to the ones who were secretly crushing back but didn't shoot their shot. Oh, and let's not forget that one crush we turned down because, well, we just weren't feeling it.

To our exes, who unknowingly fueled some of the stuff in this book, but sorry, folks, you became exes before we could give this book to you. Oops!

And hey, to the 99+ noona and oppas in our fantasies, thanks for showing up in our dreams like the stars you are!

ACKNOWLEDGEMENT

We extend our gratitude to the following individuals:

Engr. Dyñel Ortiz, for illustrating the Idyllic book cover.

Benjane Albarracin Loquinario and Engr. Katherine Ruth Miranda, who paved the way to assemble and complete the team for the *Idyllic* book project, the first-ever book project of Litras Community.

D.K. Kuizon, for making the writing process challenging and fun with his corny jokes and crazy puns.

Sol de Litras (Judy Ann L. Siasol), the visionary founder and chairperson of Litras Community, for her relentless dedication to the literary community and her instrumental role in bringing this anthology to fruition.

Lastly, to the Almighty One, who made all things possible, as stated in Philippians 4:13: *"I can do all things through Christ who strengthens me."* His grace and guidance have brought our words to life.

Contents

Author – Andrew La Balak

Breakfast

Burning bread,
Soft meals of lead.

Mornings with you,
The road ahead.

Winds of whisper,
Gusts of hair.

Your warm atmosphere,
Your bewildering air.

Grass ever-growing,
Puppies of gold.

To be with you,
Both young and old.

3

Sheets

Good morning, dearest, I just wanted to say
How perfect is the harmony when you walk and sway.

Golden is the moment when I'm with you
And to die with you is what I pray.

Long are the nights when our skin don't meet
And empty is my life when I wake up alone the next day.

Good morning, dearest, I just wanted to say
With me, on this bed, let's stay.

Bedside

Your dress of gold that flows into the misty streets of rome.

Into your brown eyes of sugary sweetness, my mind will always roam.

Built upon this poem is the savory goodness of our embrace as we sleep in my ancient foam.

My love, my love. Your sweet, sweet melody is the map that leads me back home.

5

Pot

You're like the eyes of evening sky
Bearing down on me from on high.

Many a days shall this heart of mine sunder
From your gentle waves of rolling thunder.

Wide eyes of brown does my mind long to see,
Oh, when will you come to me?

Earthen skin and plump lips of glitter.
Til then, on my tongue shall only rest bitter.

Bed

Your burning hair has filled the empty spaces of my mind.

Never have I known that I was always blind.

The cracks of my dusty heart were mended by your glorious laugh.

Why oh why did you set me on this path?

Heavenly delights and delectable sweets.

our eyes fill my mind just like how your perfume fills my sheets.

7

Summer breeze

Modern language, suits of fine silk.
Each moment with you is like a glass of warm milk.

Holding your hand and empty streets.
I'll travel the world with you, worn out feet.

Dancing in the sun, cute babies in the summer.
Every day, it gets better and better.

Cupcake

The sea, the sea. All places and roads.
All highways, all destinies, my warm abode.

My sweet, my nectar. My candlestick cold.
My fingers intertwined, my heart still holds.

All of the stars, and all of the flowers,
They scream your name with whispers of power.

Evening air, and burning moonlight.
Familiar and new, it feels so right.

9

Haiku

A haiku, a poem.
My words, my language, my heart.
Surrendered for you.

Daisies

The color of your hair has touched the deepest parts of my being.

Your gentle moves taught my soul how to sing.

Your silent melodies made me recall memories of precious sting.

The music from your body has allowed me to contemplate every little thing.

11

Desserts

Vanilla cake and other tender things.
Oh, the goodness your beauty brings.
Your gorgeous smile is the melody my heart sings.
Vanilla cake and other tender things.
For you, my dear, I would do most anything.

Breeze

Summer paradise
Heavenly songs and melodies
All of them are you.

13

Snacks

Burger Stands in the middle of the night.
A radiant smile that puts paintings to flight.
Come at me, my love. Break me with all your might.

Street Sign

Lips of pillow, morning goodness.
Noon time rush, your precious likeness.

Roads of traffic noise, city ever restless.
Stillness ever alluding, droplets of time that you bless.

Minutes pass by like leaves of gold.
You're like a ray of sunshine, most precious to behold.

15

Melt

You and I, we've seen it all.
Every brink, every sky, every hall.

Let's fade together in this darkness,
Rock along as you swallow me with your goodness.

Let's choose now the fate in which we'll thrive.
Doesn't matter where, so long as together we'll arrive.

Modern and old, familiar and new.
Golden one, precious gift, my one and only you.

Burnt

Of candles and matchsticks that litter the floor.
The misty smell of incense that clung to the door.
Moments with you, I want to make more.

17

Spotlight

All my power and all my fight.
My peace, my strength, my burning rage.

Take them all, accept them.
Restrain me, subdue me, put me in a cage.

The world is our audience,
Our love is our stage.

You've tamed me, you've calmed me.
You're my unknown, my blank page.

The Baby, The Boy, The Man

Time will come when a babe of red will you hold in your hands.

Cries of gold will whisper he. Empty is his mind, like the ground on which you stand.

Time will come when a boy of yellow will you look in the eye.

Questions of life will he ask you. Soul that wanders, his heart yearns to fly.

Time will come when a man of blue will you hold in your heart.

Embrace you, he will. You will journey with him, never shall you part.

19

Braided

Daisies fill my mind
As your skin shines in the dark.
You are my salvation,
My saving arc.

You have left me speechless,
On me, you've left your mark.

Haze

Hazy corners bent asunder.
Streets that have seen evil and plunder.
This table we share with bread and powder.
Our beating hearts of shouting thunder.

21

Fog

My clearest mind, free of dirt and fog.
The angry sound of a frustrated hug.
This morning's coffee our empty mug.

Foam

Burning embers of your
Hair have found their
Way to my innermost bones.

My soul and my mind,
I hear their cries,
I hear their groans.

My dear, my love,
Cold beer every night.
Lovely company and ice cream cones.

23

Morning

You're the morning mist that clings to the streets.
Yours is the shine of man's daring feats.
Burned in my mind, like the early morning clouds.
With you, to infinity, I am bound.

Noon

You are to me as pain is to the noontime sun.
This battle is fought, you have won.
As sure as the day, I surrender, I am done.

25

Night

This milky blue night that hangs above.
Ghostly children, flying about like doves.
This still moment with you, my only love.

Twilight

Tall grass on either sides.
What secrets they must hide.
I give you my love, I give you my pride.

Author – Dyñel Ortiz

I Will Love You Afraid

Of course, there is fear;
Of being swallowed by uncertainty
And taken to places of never-been

It's like I'm being led to a field of roses blindfolded
Certain of both the flower and the thorn
And yet unsure of the steps I will take

But I will gladly twirl in that field for you
I will sway to the music while suspended in tightrope
Guided only by the lines you draw

I will pirouette through supernovas
And waltz against gravity
For you are my love affair, and I will stay

Darling, I will love you afraid.

Sensitive

I take full ownership of my sensitive heart
It is both a blessing and a curse

And if in every universe
I get to hurt as easily as I get to love,
then so be it.
Isn't it powerful to feel
for people and things and causes
beyond ourselves?

Tongues

You built me a fortress out of paragraphs,
simply because you understood.
That I am a spirit who refuses to be tamed,
by careless tongues and its brotherhood.

31

Wildfires

You ignited my love
Like you're not afraid of wildfires.

Soft Landing

How well does he know me, I wondered.

Well enough to know
how often I have dreamt
of a soft place to land,
and how he has prepared exactly that for me.

33

Pages

And for the first time,
in a very long time,
I'm starting to fill my pages again.

The Moment I Knew

T'was the morning after a storm
And the clouds where gloomy and gray
The flowers bloomed in downcasted form
Yet my world was warm, sunny, and gay

T'was on my way home from work
As I drive down the winding road
I thought of you and gave a smirk
Yet deep inside, I'm set to explode

T'was on nights that we talked for hours
How I hung on to your every word
You had me wrapped around your stories, stares, and prayers
A dying star's wish, at last, has been heard

Awakening

After all that had come and gone
At long last, my soul has found itself undone
Revived through an ethereal renaissance
Of a lover's subliminal glance

Pirouette

Your existence had me dancing
In places where I used to tiptoe.

37

Afternoons

To love you feels like one of those afternoons
when the windows leak of radiant gold;
It fills the room with nostalgic tunes
Of all the ardent promises untold

To love you feels like one of those afternoons
when the breeze delicately echoes light;
like honey dripping from a silver spoon,
or a pair of knots untied

To love you feels like one of those afternoons
When the sun softly kisses the world goodbye;
It whispers tales of thirteen moons
and sings of unsung lullabies

Tangles

Take me to unfiltered spaces
Show me all your tangled mess
Babe, we don't have to make sense of it all.

39

August

August,

Aren't you supposed to be for the melancholy

And yet, you sang of golden tunes that burned me

You had my soul wrapped in the softness of your light

As a stranger's hand and mine, intertwined

De nouveau

Love came back with a stranger's face,
In a place that I have never been.

It knocked on my door on a summer's day,
At a time when winter's all I've seen.

Lie Naked

Let us lie naked under the stars tonight,
By that I mean, let us take off each other's masks
That we wear to hide the scars
Let us crumble before each other's eyes
Underneath this star-lit sky
And explore each other's minds
Into such depths where even our greatest fears reside

Let us lie naked under the stars tonight,
And give each other more than just peak of what we are
And as we do, the moon will sing us a lullaby
The stars will give their loudest sighs
And the universe above us will smile
As two unlikely people lie naked
For the first time, in a very long while

Lie Naked

Lightning strikes the earth at every beat
Of my longing heart, there I plant the seed
Morphing fiery veins into an eternal creed
I think of you every moment I breathe

43

Hold Still

So this is what it's like
To wake up to the warmth of your breath
And greet the sun's morning rays
Wrapped around your gentle embrace

I dare not move in hope that I freeze time
To delay slumber lifting from your eyes
And in these few, delicate moments I take my time to memorize
How your hair coils through every strand

I familiarize myself with the way your lashes flutter
And how your lips tenderly curl
I revel in the melody of your thudding heart
And how it's gloriously and precariously mine

I lift my gaze to your lovely face
And I wonder what I might have done right
That the universe allowed me the privilege

To be beheld you and be it the first thing I sight

By the Lake

Grassy banks and falling leaves
Creating rings of singing ripples
Lilies float with the gentle cold breeze
As two pairs of hands caress and fiddle

The clock ticks, but time froze
For the young lovers in the meadow
His jet-black hair and her cheeks of rose
Sing tales of eternity and tomorrow

Perfectly mine

Nightly serenades of echoing laughter
As fingertips run the curves of her spine
We trace our lives in our heads that perfect summer
She is love, made perfectly mine

47

Ill-equipped

Once, I fell in love with a painter
So I picked up a brush and learned the magic of colors
In the hopes that he'd see the art that I do
And eventually fall for me too

Then, I fell in love with a musician
So I learned to pluck my heart out on a guitar string
Sing the tunes of my love for him with a piano
But still, all my efforts have been for nought

Finally, I fell in love with a lover
Whose kindness and compassion I admire with quiet wonder
Who made me gaze upon the girl in mirror
And convinced me of all the ways I could love her better

Edges

My throat tightens at the sight of you
Holding the assembled pieces of my broken past
It isn't much, but it's all I am
Perilous yet fragile as fractured glass

I stand in awe at the sight of you
As you wrap my edges in your arms
You hold these fragments with gentle certainty
As if they're not sharp enough to bring you harm

I surrender myself at the touch of you
In your palms, I rest my heart
I will let you bind my pieces in tongues of poetry
Out of me, darling, I will let you make art

Wave after wave

Have you ever seen the sun beneath the waves
Iridescent honey gold against the blue
Ethereal fire reaching for the ocean caves
Darling, it is in such magic that I love you

Distance and Daydreams

What better way to spend an afternoon
Than with blank pages by the lake
I dream and draw a life with you
Until this longing heart ceases to ache

51

A Thousand Little Things

A thousand little stories
And a thousand little songs
Yet I couldn't capture you in a thousand little poems

A thousand little paintings
More than a thousand little art
Yet no canvas can ever hold the beauty and the grandeur of your heart

Home

I have been in places where I don't belong
Like indecisive hearts and crowded streets
For a time, I'm convinced that I'm in the wrong
For having edges that don't seem to fit

Until one night as I walk under lilac lights
I heard a faint whisper of a lullaby
And as I stepped into the rhythm of the night
I saw you there singing the song of my heart's battlecry

You took me by the hand and sang me of more songs
Of tales of your adventures, and of the places you have roamed
We have been in places where we don't belong
And now, at last, we have found ourselves a home

The Museum

I walk through empty hallways
With my heart on my hands
As I search for the perfect artwork
Of which my soul had long demand

I thought I knew what I was looking for
An art with a shade of blue
A piece that will drown me in it oceans
I thought it's where my heart is true

I search through empty hallways
Desperate at every turn
To beheld the perfect artwork
That will make my soul burn

I look through empty hallways
Wondering if I'll ever find
The art that will tell my story
The art that I had in mind

As I walk through empty hallways
A light had caught my eye
I turned to see where it came from
And all I could do was sigh

There, I stand upon an artwork
Made of strokes so bold
I never thought it possible
An art like this could be told

It does not show a hint of blue
But of hues that is yet to be found
It does not tell my story
And it cannot make me drown

I stand upon a painted hallway
And thought not of yesterdays
For the work tells not of my story
But the future of my days

I stand upon a painted hallway
My soul excited, my heart in awe
And yet, I thought it as surreal

Unable to fully grasp what I saw

I stand upon a painted hallway
With a heart full of pride
For painted in that artwork
Is the world seen from your eyes

Author – Sweet Cold Ruth

57

Your Warmth and I

The sun may never grasp your gentle warmth,
Nor shall the breeze whisper of your peace,
And though no one ever will,
I, on the other hand, have grown fond of it.

Nature may never know how I've grown with you,
And neither will the flowers see how I've beautifully bloomed,
And though no one ever will,
I, on the other hand, have come to love myself for it.

Dance

Delicate hearts entwined with a single glance
As weary and once-lost souls found romance.
Nurtured by a rhythm's sweet, gentle trance,
Cherished moments, each fleeting chance,
Each dance, our souls tenderly advance.

Symphony

Ours is a love that the heavens crafted,
Our own masterpiece endlessly painted,
A lovely song or poem in perfect rhyme,
A pillar of peace that stood through time.

Ours is a symphony that will never cease
A melodious written verse with lovely beats
And I, the conductor, find my place in you
Guiding our love, like a maestro in pursuit.

Joy in Rain

For what is rain but your warmth's comfort?
That though sorrow gently falls upon my face,
Your love radiates joy my heart knew not of.

Spring Bloom

In spring's tender breeze,
Love unfolds like a spring bloom.
Petals unfurling,
Its fragrant embrace, divine.
Life's sweetest dream, forever mine.

Let Me

If the world crushed your soul before you could even build your tower,

Let me be the fortress that shields you from their power.

Allow me to be the light they relentlessly stole from you,

Let me be the beacon that guides you through every darkest hour.

63

A Tale Retold

In the shadowed pages of my past,
I wrote a tale of sorrow, meant to last.
With ink of tears and a heavy heart,
I penned a story in papers torn apart.

But then you came, a gentle breeze,
Whispering love through ancient trees.
Your touch, a balm for scars so deep,
Awakening a love forever put to sleep.

No longer bound by chains of despair,
You mended my heart with tender care.
In your embrace, I found my way,
To sunlit skies and a brand-new day.

Love, a remedy for wounds of old,
A narrative rewritten, a tale retold.
With you, I've learned to truly see,
The happy ending that was meant to be.

Love Remained Forever Still

Love cradles you in your darkest hours,
Finds beauty amidst your chaos,
And cherishes you, flaws and all.

Love is that blazing fire in joy,
But it is also that faint ember
When hope seems lost.

Love lets you explore and wander;
Love is a warm hug waiting for you
To come home when the search is over.

Love remained forever still
In this ever-changing world,
And love will always be you.

I Fear, Dearest

I fear with great depth, dearest–
How possible love can easily be let go,
And it terrifies me even more–
How grand the love I bear be wasted.

I fear with great unease, dearest–
How you've made me breathe your air,
Thoughts keep me wide awake at night–
How my world suffocates without you.

I fear with great despair, dearest–
That if my hands no longer feel yours,
My heart will cease to genuinely beat,
My mind, a restless search for peace.

You alone, love, hold my sanity;
You alone can put my chaos to rest,
So hold me and prove that love can last;
Hold me tight and bury my fears to past.

To Future from Past

In you, I found the bridge that spans the years,
A love that overcame the past's numbed tears.
You're the reason the waiting was not for naught,
The missing piece my soul has long sought.

Through countless days, my heart knew no reprieve
'Til you arrived and once more, made me believe.
And now, I see why the past bathed me in blue,
For it was the only way fate could lead me to you.

Only the heavens know how long I have waited,
How I resorted to the thought of my luck ill-fated,
And yet, here, you now hold me in your arms,
The answer to prayers, my ever-lucky charm

In your embrace, I've found my home at last,
A love that's timeless, to future from past.

Hidden

You were there when I wrote them for you,
How I explained what each symbol meant,
Those words cryptically etched on the board,
I saw you light up as you read and understood.

And yet, my notebook hid what I could not convey,
Same symbols, but truer words I wish I could say,
But I froze at your smile as I taught you my very weakness,
For if you saw what was hidden, I am forever doomed helpless

How Clumsy of a Clever Girl

You are bright and ever amusing,
And I bask in my own darkness.
While you be tainted by my hue,
I bathe myself in your kindness.

Gently flows the river your peace brings.
Bright are the mornings with your smiles.
Dreary are the days of your absence.
Arid is the breeze without your laughter.

I began to fear a world without your beauty.
I have become entangled in such weakness.
How clumsy of a clever girl to cave in,
But I cannot afford to lose sight of you.

So shine, I dare say, though it is bad for me.
You are my Achilles' heel; I shall melt away.
Stay–that is my one and only request.
Be the light in my cold and dark world.

Define You

Perfectly kept memories of you on display,
For every quirk, a cherished work of art,
In laughter lines and the way they convey,
Your love's true song, a symphony at heart.

The way you joyfully dance to the beats
Or sing off-tune without one care sought.
For moments you had one song on repeat
Or stared blankly at walls in deep thought.

In each whim, a glimpse of you shines
Like a child so lively, ever ready to tease
Or a youthful soul aging like fine wine,
A mosaic of uniqueness, a masterpiece,

So let each quirk define your radiant star,
And know I will always love all that you are.

Calm

You, my home, bring peace;
Warm sunlight within your hold,
Storms calm at one touch.

Lullaby

What an amusing fate we must have
That the heavens designed our union,
That though we braved stormy seas,
A single touch made all make sense.

You lulled my worries to restful sleep
And hushed demons that whispered.
You planted gardens in arid desserts
And drowned the blazing pain away.

Weak

Truth be told, I'm better alone
In fact, I am stronger alone.
But with you around, I am weak,
And I guess that's the beauty in it.

Because with you, I can be weak.
I am free to be vulnerable.
I am allowed to be frail,
And my fragile heart is honored.

And if being strong means forgetting
That I, too, need to be saved,
Then just on some days with you,
I am at peace being weak.

Air

Grocery bags and heavy machines,
All these things I maneuver with ease.
Heartbreaks and problems at hand,
No worries too great of a demand.

Been through the worst, been through it all,
Both knees on the ground at fate's cruel call,
But then you came, and the narrative changed.
You carried the burdens and erased all pain.

And suddenly, everything felt light like air,
Then it hit me–I no longer have to walk alone.
The past holds no chains against my sanity;
The nightmares no longer choke the life out.

And you–you who saved me–I can't thank you enough;
I can't praise the heavens enough for the gift of you.
The long-awaited prayer has been answered.
You have found me, and I, you. I am forever grateful.

Clouds

Your phone painted the sky that day
As clouds followed you all around.
Love so warm like a soft embrace,
Cuddling me in your arms of peace.

Watch them drift and dance away
As we reminisce the love we found
Like the cool breeze on your face,
You, love, calm all my worries at ease.

Drafts and Pages

These drafts and pages can never hold
The moments shared, our stories untold.
In the spaces between these written lines,
Unfold memories and unspoken times.

This, we hold, forever etched in our hearts,
A tale of passion where our souls take part.
Words may fade as the pages grow old,
But our love blazes bright, forever bold.

Beyond the sorrows of life, we find our way,
Going home to a familiar warmth day by day.
With every page turned, every draft revised,
Our story continues to breeze through life,

For it's not the ink on the paper's face,
Nor the photos that have been saved
That immortalize what we have right here;
It is but our promise held through the years.

77

Drafts and pages may come and go,
Yet our story, forever an eternal glow.

You Make Me

You make me forget, love,
Every ache, every blaring noise,
And I have grown tired of the old.
With you, I forget them all, love.

You make me cheerful, love.
No pain, not even one misery
Can ever cloud the joy you give,
And yes, you make me cheerful.

You make me wonder, love
Of how you found your way to me;
My heart knew only of sorrows,
And yet, you make me wonder.

You make me question, love,
Every doubt that once held sway.
With you, every uncertainty fades,
And confidence finds its way home.

79

You make me remember, love,
The beauty that's found in today.
Your eyes hold reflections of joy,
A silent hope, forever here to stay,

So, I question no more, love.
Doubts dissipate like morning mist.
For in your presence, dearest,
Certainty finds its home, gently kissed.

The Child in Me

The child in me dances in joy
As you cradle my yearning heart.
The chaos in me strides to end
As you hold my storm in order.

The child in me unlearns the world
As you detangle every single string
That caused my weary feet to trip;
You silence every bit of cacophony.

The child in me feels safe by your side,
In the haven of your steadfast embrace.
As you shelter me from raging tempests,
A sanctuary where love fills the air.

And, love, the child in me is happy,
Wrapped in the gentle glow of your care.
All because of you, who hold the key,
To where childhood dreams still dare.

Lies and Truths

I've heard all lies, both heartbreaking and beautiful.
Felt betrayed by the people kept closest to my side,
Deceit somehow became a familiar tune to my ears,
A dissonant melody that never spoke of peace.

Guarded was my feeble heart which had suffered damage;
Terrified was I that each nightmare might happen again,
And yet, something tells me that you're worth the shot;
Something tells me fate might end differently with you.

Finally, I met a soul that doesn't lie to deceive me,
Shall I risk my sanity, or shall I now risk all for you?
In your eyes, I have found one truth ever so rare.
In your love, my heart learned to trust once more.

Tempest

I have gone atrociously insane for making you my world,
What madness, what tempest to have let you in my hold.
My nights have not known quietness without your breath.
I am forever ensnared in your spell, forever latched to you.

I sleep peacefully with you by my side alone.
In the sacred silence of our shared dreams,
Where your heartbeat harmonizes with mine,
I have gone mad, dearest–all because of your love.

Quills on Parchments

In the bygone echoes of yesteryears,
Where quills danced on parchments,
Our love was bathed in sepia hues,
An ancient sonnet, an ageless page.
As moonlit ink traced our tender tale,
Each phrase a serenade, each word a spell.

From rhythms to free-versed poems,
My heart learned the ways you spoke.
Language may be rewritten over time
In the sands of evolving tongues,
Yet, in every whisper of the wind,
Our love remains, a timeless song.

Set in Stone

So let me write these thoughts before I lose
The exact words to describe this love so rare.
Let me capture in ink what my heart can't refuse,
Every precious moment we've held with care,

And let me set in stone the love I saved for you,
The exact feelings I so wrongly gave the world,
Realizing it was only you who deserved such a gem,
Ever broken, but ever ready to finally love you right.

Author – Sol de Litras

Plaid Trousers

Oh, my lady in plaid trousers shine,
Thy radiant smile, a fine wine.

In a world once veiled, now bathed in light,
Crisped brown locks, akin not to Dwight.

Oh, my lady in plaid trousers elite tete,
Thine almond eyes, meeting streetlight greet.

Keen observers in my soul's passé,
She sees through glitters, pretense kept gray.

Oh, my lady in plaid trousers true,
Nay prying questions, understands one of deux.

By the cellar where honesty is stored,
She stands firm, emotions never hoard.

Oh, my lady in plaid trousers dear,

87

Soft and quaint, thine hand sincere.

A reassuring grasp yond all shall be in line,
In thy touch, a gage, sweet and benign.

Sea Child

On the shore, where waves do tenderly kiss the sand,
A child, nay longer at youth's strict command,
Gazes at the vast, open sky of July,
Then turns to the sea of memories—whys and sighs:

"Love not like the sun's fierce light,
'Tis scorching rays, a bewildering fight,
For in its blaze, a path lost in endless noon,
Blinds and blinds, till freedom is doom.
Oh so, know my child, listen well and see,
Love like the moon, gentle and free."

Those were her father's short words,
Before the sea ended his birth in the north port.

Maybe

They spoke of farewells can be a gentle tune,
Maybe akin to how we bid adieu under the moon,
And the soft rustle of leaves replaced by tender kisses,
With coir ashes turned to granted wishes.

They spoke of endings, a painting of monsoon rain,
As friends, we parted, like rice fields in golden grain.
The story of us, rewritten and gently it smitten,
More than the mountains, it never frightens, it fountains.

Maybe, yond's how rises hums the ends of its own,
And the spice arises from dusk to dawn.

Maybe, despite the drought brought by summer,
We spend time with lime or buko in the Pasig river—
Under a coconut tree on white sand beaches,
Where the waft softly bruits gentle stitches.
Maybe, despite the floods in the wet seasons,

We find comfort in a robusta coffee session,
Listening to the stomping of rain on nipa hut's cover,
Each stomp bewrays a story yond can't be smother.

Maybe, just maybe, farewells, as we find,
Aren't as heavy, thou see, endings can be kind.

Country Girl

To my soul mate, here I write my longing,
By the sea where mountains are blending.

In this Pearl of the Orient Sea where we stood alone,
Will there be dawn at which hour our love finds its home?

I seek thy flesh offered by carabao mango trees,
But am alarmed by how their fruits can be sweet,
Outshining even the gust of the calamay treat.

Art thou among these folks, or hath fate not set?
I wonder thy journey, silhouette begets.

I wonder if thou'rt a tango of crickets brave and rare,
I wonder if thou'rt a song sung by maya birds in the air,
Or a ukulele yond strums tales of love with flair.
Just know, I'm here, waiting, without fear,

For the day our paths align, drawing thee near.

93

Graffiti

In the street that greet and meet colorful arts,
I felt like the city's graffiti yond was seen by every heart.
Passerby’s behold at me, try to understand,
But only a few really get why I was made as I am.

Oh, Vicente, My Own Father!

Oh, Vicente, my own father!
Love is not a game of deceit and lies,
Nor a cruel mask in a lover's guise.

Oh, Vicente, my own father!
Love is not a bilboes yond holds one bound,
Or a prison where one's dreams are drowned.

Oh, Vicente, my own father!
Love is not a fire yond engluts with rage,
But a gentle warmth in a frozen stage.

Oh, Vicente, my own father!
Love is a language yond needs nay words,
A mixture of feelings yond gently stirs.

Oh, Vicente, my own father!
Love is forgiving, it mends each scar,
An antidote that heals, near or far

95

Oh, Vicente, my own father!
Love is fierce sirius, burning bright,
With a pole star in the dunnest night.

Paws

Offstage of woofs and meows,
With each bark and purr yond vows—
Hoomans scratch their heads, don't get our game,
But making thee nimble-footed, oh, ‘tis not the same!

I throw a ball when thou art in a purring spree,
But truth be told, 'tis thy purr-sonality I want to see.

Thou lick thy fur, and I do the same,
Mirror, mirror, in this fur-fun game.

Day and night, different as I can be,
But in thy look, I find glee.

Thou groom with thy tongue, oh, what a sight—
A fur-tastic prance, a joy so right.

In snug nooks, we share a treat or two,
Not just playmates, but cozy buddies too.

So, here's to us, in our whimsical feat,
A quirky paw story—sweet is't not, this gentle treat?

Haven

Let the world judge, it won't deter,
I've found a haven with thee, yond's for sure.

If They Wished

If they wished, they would,
Master the art of serenade,
Though thine ears and tongue be ailing.

If they wished, they would,
Carve out time for thee,
Where moments find their way.

If they wished, they would,
Attain thee, unfazed by distance,
Be it through air, land, or sea.

If they wished, they would,
Comprehend flaws 'neath concealers,
And the skin of thine bosom's bloom.

If they wished, they would,
Write love letters beyond courtship,
But in endless days.

If they wished, they would,
Declare love not solely in words,
But in deeds, heard and seen.

If they wished, they would,
Tarry not, but patiently linger
For thy presence, so dear.

If they wished, they would,
Ne'er turn away, for they would ne'er,
Leave thee in the first place.

101

Home

I am yond maiden of college days;
Who oft desired to flee home,
Yet now, a mother awaiting
The homeward path:
French kisses to simple joys,
Now kindle my delight;
From sumptuous feasts to—
home-baked treats with children.

Aye, in days of yore,
A lass with dreams to roam;
But anon, a homemaker crafting my abode,
And at last, within the bosom of home.

Only

Oh lonely glows, at night only know,
How I long for thy sweet caress to show.

Oh holy astral, at dark skies only arise,
Witness the fondness yond continually hides.

Oh ghostly fluff, only drifts and sighs,
Swallows secrets of sorrows when I cry.

Oh yowly mizzle, only falls unseen and free,
Accept the depth of my love for thee.

Oftentimes

Oftentimes, I ponder, lost in thought,
What occupies thy mind, what's sought?

Oftentimes, I muse, in moments still,
What resides within, what's thy will?

Oftentimes, I wonder, without a fuss,
What bridges the space between us?

Tinikling

Tap-tap, like raindrops on a tin roof,
He spies her through the bamboo's aloof.

Rat-a-tat, as the sticks gently swoon,
His lips hum an awe-struck tune.

Snap-snap, like a river's playful tide,
His jaw drops as her nimble feet glide.

Her feet sputter, a subtle flutter,
His heartbeat thunders like a proud lover.

Taste buds

Love resembles taste buds keen,
Thou savor not just sweetness serene.
But also the salty, bitter, and sour,
And at times, love's taste be plain, yet dour.

New Chapter

Is it amiss to love more than one in a lifetime's span?
If 'tis, then deem me wrong for cherishing you,
After I closed the chapter of once I held dear.

Destiny

Crowded jee, brief glimpse,
Eyes meet in fleeting whelm,
Akin to a film.

In rushed, hushed coffee shops,
Folks poised, chat, some rejoice,
By chance, fingers touch.

Work's looming deadline,
Mates find more, fate's subtle call,
Office door's knock falls.

So, destiny swifts.
Not in grand plans, but serene,
Moments softly sigh.

Kindergarten

With a smirk, he shared his eraser with mine,
A gesture simple, one I could not decline.

Kindness revealed in ABC walls,
A silent language, truths and false calls.

I clutched the eraser, a treasure to behold,
Rhyming in corners of maroon and gold.

On the playground where laughter took flight,
Hand in hand, our worlds felt just right.

Together we played on the see-saw and in screams,
Innocence lit, dreams sparkled in streams.

Shared hotcakes at snack time, friendship so dear,
In the kingdom of building blocks, we engineer.

A confession in a game of pretend,

"*I like thee,*" he said, a message to send.

Naivety wrapped around our tiny fingers,
Crayon drawings turned into letters.

A stolen kiss on a cheek, shy and sweet,
Parents teased us when we did meet.

What is Love?

'Neath the sun with eight rays, golden and true,
Santan's red blooms, sampaguitas in the afternoon's hue.

On a carabao's back, my spirit soar,
Brown skin glistening, in the humid Kore.

A blend of garlic, soy sauce, and bay leaves wafts,
Spellbound, I trail the fragrance as it drafts.

To a quaint nipa hut, where lamplight beams,
A wedded twain welcomed me, fulfilling dreams.

"Dong, good afternoon, join us for an early dinner," they said,
A greeting of warmth, as the sun dipped and bled.

Amid the molave table, carved by time's design,
I turned to my carabao 'neath the moon's gentle shine.

111

I watched as he put adobo on her China plate,
I started contemplating loves ponderous weight.

"What is love?" I queried the wedded twain,
They gazed, smiles pure and unfeigned.

I ceased to question, for on their faces, I can see,
Love is beyond definition, ageless, and remains ever free.

With Thee

When I'm with thee, I find,
Angels grace my jumbled mind;
The galaxy sparkles in my eyes,
And the stars, once sprinkled, align in the skies.

Party

In the party, where not-so-me wants to play,
I quaffed a blend of cocktails, forth and back, I swayed.

My lips smirked, and my hips slayed,
My eyes gazed, waiting for my prey.

Down my throat, its essence flowed,
A libation for words in my heart bestowed.

For the unspoken feelings, I sought reprieve,
A truth concealed, my soul grieved.

I yearned to utter, face to face,
The confessions yond my heart weighs.

Yet, the words I'd planned to set adrift,
Buried deep, a secret gift.
'Neath the crescent's glow, as stars withdrew,

"I profess my love unto thee," I whispered to a few.

Not solely to thee, my beautiful delight,
But to the night, and the stars so bright.

115

Like a Cat

A cat came nigh unto me,
Its steps unheard, silent as can be.

Its presence went unnoticed at first,
For I was absorbed in other matters.

Until, I was shocked—
Wherefore, oh wherefore,
Art thou anon in my lap?

Wherefore, oh wherefore,
Hast thou become a part of me?

Wherefore, oh wherefore, like a cat—
Yond's how thou came into my life.

Dram Bee

In yonder garden, where I unfurled,
A dram bee, swift, upon my petal twirled.

Have mercy, for he sought my cherished bloom!
Have mercy, fearing he'd gather pollen's plume!

Yet, the gardener cautioned against hasty disdain,
For the bee's sting, a part of his essence, not in vain.

In this garden of wisdom, I discerned,
Needed, not just wanted, the lesson learned.

Now, I yield to his proboscis meant,
And accept his buzzing consent.

117

Fallen

I've fallen for—
Thine eyes, which shine through
The flood of sunlight.

I've fallen for—
Thine big, bold smile, full of pride
And courageous might.

I've fallen for—
Thine sheer goodness makes waters
Run clear and bright.

I've fallen for—
Thine thoughts light up
The side of marias sight.

I've fallen for—
Thine spirit spins above
The tops of the skyscrapers' height.

I've fallen for—
Thine heart touches the lonely cries,
Casting a gentler fight.

Durian

A durian, a boon from the ties of connubial bliss,
Laid bare in mine own hands. Already undone.

Its naked allure beckoned, a tempting vision yond—
Spake of enticements veiled in ripened layers.

As I cradled its yielding flesh,
A tender touch disclosed the softness beneath,
A revelation of concealed desires.

The fragrance, bold and alluring,
Lured me into an exploration of senses.

I leaned in, a pledge of ecstasy upon mine lips,
And dared to partake the inaugural caress,
An ingress into forbidden sonnets and covert cravings.

Each twirl played upon mine buds, a troupe of pleasure,

Yond left me yearning for more.

When I Am Not With Thee

When I'm not with thee, as time denies,
Let's wander through moments, our love ties.

From CIT-University's study area where first we met,
To midnight strolls on Osmeña Boulevard fret.

Confessions faltered, both nervous and teary,
Wordless, thou just hugged me dearly.

Our wedding, 'neath the Cathedral's twilight glee,
Thou in white lace, my heart sworn wholly to thee.

In laughter and sorrow, midst children's joyous cheer,
Through chaos and clamor, our bond held ever near.

Recall yond eve, in the kitchen's lively spree,
Pizza dough skirmishes, flour-stained esprit.

When words, sharp swords in heated exchange,

Yet forgiveness bloomed, a slate to rearrange.

Amid sniffles and tissues, midst the trial's grip,
Side by side, we faced it with unyielding fellowship.

From paychecks in plenty to the canned sardines,
Hand in hand, we held each other, enjoying the scenes.

Under rain's soft patter, hand in hand we'd waltz,
We dance, not for gain, but for shared exalts.

As the bedside clock ticks, and shadows draw near,
Let gratitude eclipse the impending tear.

No need for farewells, just a brief parting, dear,
In the next life, where our love shalt reappear.

About the Authors

Andrew La Balak

Andrew La Balak is currently immersed in the world of academia as a student pursuing a Bachelor of Arts in Linguistics at the University of San Carlos. Beyond the academic corridors, he is a fusion of a Cebuano *mambabalak* and a true-blue aspiring traditional artist.

Dyñel Ortiz

Dyñel Ortiz is an alumna of the University of San Carlos, where she earned her degree in Civil Engineering and subsequently became a registered civil engineer. Outside her professional pursuits, she indulges in her artistic inclinations, showcasing a unique talent for both visual arts and the written word.

Sweet Cold Ruth

Sweet Cold Ruth is a Cebu-based civil engineer and an alumna of the University of San Carlos. Apart from writing, she is a music enthusiast who has a passion for singing and rapping. She's also an educator, tackling subjects like Math, Science, SAT, IELTS, English, and Reading. Her writing usually delves into genres revolving about love, faith, life, duality (e.g. darkness and light). Her writing style usually uses metaphors and other literary devices.

Sol de Litras

Sol de Litras is a passionate enthusiast in street photography, arts and crafts, and writing. She is an alumna and a dedicated full-time faculty member at the Cebu Institute of Technology-University. With co-authorship contributions to numerous anthology books, Sol de Litras exemplifies versatility and creativity in her writing style.

www.ingramcontent.com/pod-product-compliance
Lightning Source LLC
La Vergne TN
LVHW091530070526
838199LV00001B/8
9789362698018